SCAVENGERS AMONG US

Written and illustrated by Tim Wentz

Thanks to my loving wife
for enduring long hours of
my writing and her support

ISBN # 978-0-615-26439-4

Acknowledgment to my family members , who have struggled with many financial issues and hardships in their lives , while teaching the younger ones life values and opportunities .
Trials and tribulations witnessed personally have inspired me to write this book, so that all families may benefit and prosper . A big thank you to my close family members who over the years , have supported each other in ventures , happy or sad .

Persons , places and scenarios mentioned here in are illustrated solely as an educational example and not intended to reveal a family or to cause harm in any way . Reference to family members such as cousins, aunts , uncles and grandparents are only used as a training plot to converge the important messages of this book.

Disclaimer Note

Tim Wentz is not a tax or legal advisor . The tools and guidelines used in this publication are solely suggested and are not factual . Although the general financial scenarios when applied correctly and in a conservative way are beneficial for an investment program . Results can vary depending on investments , rates and type of programs . The information given here is designed to help you make informed decisions about your finances and assets .
Please consult with a competent tax and/or legal advisor for your specific situation .

Dedicated to my
Father and Mother
for their support,
enthusiasm,
and love

We love our family and friends . Our parents have worked hard all of their lives to provide a good life for us as we were growing up . They took care of us when we were sick and injured . We had a nice roof over our heads and we lived very well. Our family went on nice vacations every year , yes ... we had a nice childhood !

Although this is my true life story , many do not have a nice childhood . Sad ....but true , many factors may contribute to an undesirable childhood . Money , unstable jobs , moving from job to job , unstable marriage or relationship , injury or sickness in the family , family hardships , lower family income , drug and or alcohol abuse , adoption and other misfortunes may cause a not so happy childhood .

Many families have assets in properties , personal possessions and finances . Many have considerable amount in total value , while many may not have anything of value . Example ..... if one family has a net worth of $100,000 and another family may only have $10,000 , there is still value there to protect for the future . Even if the poorest of the poor has a net worth of only $1000 , there is still a value to protect .

The reason why I wrote this book is because of a unfortunate family event that had happen to our Father and his assets

No one should have to go through what our Father , my siblings and I had to endure . Father had always felt his money was protected in the banks and he trusted in his wife to do well with monies and records . His step children was also trusted in exchange of monies and use of personal endeavors . Several events occurred in a years time to reduce my fathers assets legally in court , I legally can not reveal details , but this was real and traumatic to the family .

Our Father is alive and disagrees with many decisions made in court , but we had to negotiate to an agreement . The events and situations which lead up to the asset reduction is multiple and lengthily , a book could be written in itself , but I really can't divulge any information as there may be some final disbursements in the future .

The lawyers involved followed the marital laws with respect to both parties and children involved to reach a decision in our Fathers situation . Laws will vary from state to state . The lawyers did mention that if the assets were recorded properly and placed in safer accounts , our father wouldn't have had the problems he encountered .

I wish that by writing this book , you will take it to heart and look at your families assets . Take the first step to read this book carefully and make notes . Seriously consider your family and the protection you can provide them . Be proactive now and you and your family could save a lot of grief and possibly thousands and thousands of dollars in assets .

You are about to discuss topics to your parents that " No one likes to talk about ! " . But be strong and believe that this is the right thing to do . Openly discuss all of the reasons for what your family is going to record and trust placed upon a few members of your family .

After you and your family start talking openly about these topics , it will get easier to talk about the issues . There could be scavengers living among us , meaning if your family assets , records , wills and last wishes are not recorded properly and secured , there could be problems in the future .

Take in account that not all situations , family members and state laws are not the same . With our fathers personal struggle , we had three different lawyers tell us the same thing on several of the issues within this book . I am happy to share this information with you.

You may say that your family already has recorded and secured the important issues , but seriously look at the whole picture and protect you and your families future .

I wish you and your Family well in this important venture .

Dated : October , 29th , 2008

Sincerely ,   Tim Wentz

Resources : Lawinfo.com
          AARP
          Edward Jones

Chapters		Page

Times are tough and the American dollar isn't as valuable as it once was . Today is April the 28th , 2008 and gas is up to $3.58 a gallon and they say it could reach $ 4.00 this summer . Unbelievable ......when I graduated from high school in 1973 , gas was $ .25 a gallon . Some economists say we are in a recession , as many people are out of work and good paying jobs are hard to find , people are not spending their hard earned money foolishly .

Even college students out of school have a hard time finding good jobs. Graduates will need a bachelors or a masters degree in administration , accounting , healthcare , engineering fields as example for a good paying job.

There are speciality jobs , don't get me wrong , like a master chef , a senator , a movie star , a scientist , a film director , a great accomplished writer or musician or president of the united states. These again are a few examples and securing a good job will take hard work, great studies and the long climb up the corporate ladder.

A lot of workers live from paycheck to paycheck , especially if they are the only one bringing home the paycheck or are living alone. It really helps when there are two incomes in a household .Young workers usually don't think about starting a retirement , as there are many important things they spend their money on in their daily lives.

Although now is the time in their young working life to start investing into a retirement program. Now I have heard it said by many workers that they can't afford to save any money towards their retirement , but ... they've got it all wrong. In fact ... they can't afford NOT to invest into a retirement program. The secret is to pay yourself first !

Now we all know that we have to pay rent or a mortgage , make car payments , buy groceries , pay utilities , the important things to live . But if you work for a business or corporation that has some type of investment program for retirement , many personal choice investments are deducted from your paycheck before your income is taxed . So with this in mind , you may NOT even notice a reduction in your take home pay.

If your unsure about investing with a reputable investments company , ask your personnel department or check with a local investor brokerage or go online to investment securities . A licensed securities agent will discuss the various options with you .

And if your unsure about how much to invest per pay , start off low , like 6 % per pay . If you earn $1000 a pay and invest 6 % , that would be $ 60 a pay . Keep in mind that this is before it is taxed , so the amount will be lower than the $ 60 a pay . Now... some of you may say that you can't even afford to do that . As I said in the earlier paragraph , the secret is to pay yourself first .

What you will need to do is to look at your monthly income and monthly expenses . This is also an excellent portfolio for your budget report. You may say " who cares about a budget ", but if your one who lives from paycheck to paycheck , you may be interested in this budget .

So here is a monthly budget based on $1000 a pay at four pays a month .
Expenses are : $ 1500 mortgage , $300 car payment , $250 groceries , $200 utilities , $150 for
    insurances , $200 gas , $200 clothes and shoes , $300 credit card , $100 doctor , $100 dentist ,
    $500 entertainment , $100 savings account , $80 food at work .
    Total Expenses for a month are : $ 3980 .

This leaves only $20 left over from the month . This is obviously a tight budget and looking at the expenses for the month , there can be adjustments made to start a retirement program .
Let's take a look at where we can make adjustments to free up some money for retirement :

1. $200 gas bill for your car . With gas prices going up this is understandable . But here are some little things we can do to help. If you live close to work , walk or ride a bike to work. Car pool with someone to work or get an energy efficient vehicle or motor bike . One good thing about walking or riding a bike to work , this is good exercise and in turn could reduce your $100 doctor bill each month by the healthy exercise . You could save $50 or more here .

2. Look in detail to the entertainment expenses of $500 a month. Is this by eating out often , going to the movies , clubs , race track , parties or shows ? Consider eating out only once a week instead two or three times a week. Reduce the other fun things mentioned to minimize the costs . Look at non costly fun things like a walk in the park or woods , rent a video for at home , small private low budget parties . You could save over $100 here .

3. Food costs at work can be expensive . A cheaper alterative would be to pack your lunch from home. The extra cost on the grocery bill for packing your lunch would be cheaper than spending the money in the cafeteria . You could save easily $40 here .

As you can see , by making some adjustments in your budget , you would have the money to set aside each pay or have deducted from your pay towards a retirement program. The few changes mentioned above , saved $ 190 a month in this case . This could allow an increase from the proposed 6 % to at least a safe 12% investment .

When I started my retirement investing 30 years ago , I was like every youngster , leery about starting a retirement. Probably the money taken out of my paycheck was the number one concern, so I started with only $25 a pay. Funny thing is that the $25 taken out , I didn't even notice missing .
This went on for a few years and my portfolio wasn't growing much , so I increased it to $50 a pay .
Marriage and starting a family took priority over my thoughts of retirement , the $50 stayed withdrew each pay for many years . Then with marginal pay increases , I also increased my investments and now I am at 23% invested . This sounds very aggressive and it is indeed . This 23% has been there working for me about 8 years now and I have about ten more years to invest at this rate. It is estimated to be valued around $200,000 at retirement age. Did I mention my wife and I are retiring early ? We both have been so aggressive in investments that we can retire at the age of 62 .
My wife's portfolio is projected to be valued even more than mine is estimated to be , So we will be set very well . With this total projection , we will be able to maintain our current life style for 30 years in retirement. Although this also includes other programs like personal stocks , social security, employment pensions and savings.

Alright now .... Have I got you thinking ? I hope so . Get a pad of paper and ink pen . Write down your total monthly household incomes and then write down all of your household expenditures . Remember all of the primary ones listed on page 13 as an example . Everyone is going to have different expenditures . Hopefully yours will have a larger tally in the black than the example given . A lot of people prefer to have a cushion of money for an emergency or for a big vacation .

If expenditures exceed your incomes , then you have a big problem before you ever get started . Maybe your unemployed right now for some reason or not able to work or already retired . Maybe you're the only income in a household family . Hopefully you have supplemental incomes and already have a plan or you have a nice retirement already and are reaping the benefits . I realize that not everyone are not fortunate as others and just making ends try to meet is all they can do . Try to explore all of the options .

Be sure to contemplate your whole financial picture to see where your at exactly .
Again , I am amazed at the number of people who have NOT put the pencil to the paper and just work and live from day to day . That is sad !!

This is not that difficult to figure out . Could it be also that your one who likes toys or waste money on silly things. Do you have a bad habit that you can't seem to beat ? Like smoking , drinking or gambling ?   I use to smoke many years ago when I was young and decided it was bad and mostly.. I didn't want to raise my children around it . Enough said about life styles . Please look closely at your situation and figure out your household budget .

I hope I didn't put you sleep with this first chapter . What I wanted to do was to wake you up ! You may not think so , but this is serious business when it comes to you and your families assets .

If you are just out there having fun and not wanting to plan for your future.... your retirement , I feel sorry for you. There is a future .... a retirement .... and it has your name listed on it . Are you thinking that social security will be there for you or thinking that's my retirement ! I don't need any more ! Wrong ! Figures show you will need other accounts to maintain your current life style . Is your mortgage going to be paid off before you retire ? How about other debts ? Draw it all out on paper to see where you will be at before you retire . You should have only minor bills to keep up , like utilities, taxes , insurances , food costs , etc. ... that would be preferable. All you have to do is act on it and act now. Get the pencil going !

Just start out small on investing and see how it goes , but you have to start now !

" Many don't plan to fail , many fail to plan "

Now your ready !
Pull all of your records, papers and account books out on the table. Your going to tally up all of the savings , CD's , IRA's , pension ,social security , stocks , bonds, and any other accounts that is a financial asset .

A checking account should not be included as this will fluctuate with time as you pay bills and live off of this account in your daily life.

Personal property will now be valued and tallied up. Personal assets will be properties , vehicles , boats , lots , antiques , collections , jewelry , art work , etc. . Some assets will grow in value as time goes on , while others will depreciate in time . A fair market value will need to be determined for each item listed . A $15000 car valued as of today , which is used every day , may only be worth $1000 fifteen years from now . But an old vintage car , not driven and kept clean , dry and well maintained may be rare and very valuable fifteen years from today.

So its difficult to put a price on an item as it would depend on originality , mint condition and demand . Some items you may want appraised , like your home , art work , vehicles , etc.

You may be surprised at your total assets . If your spendable accounts come to $80,000 and a pension draw of $1100 a month and social security draw expected to be $900 a month , you may be set well for retirement. That is if you have no debts ! Also if your personal assets value total to $150,000 , then your total package will look very good .

Another person although may not have a good package at all . Their type of employment may not offer a pension at all and their spendable accounts only total $4,000 . Their social security draw is expected to be only $750 a month and they have always rented ... never owned a home ! They have large debts from credit cards and their personal assets value is estimated to be $20,000 .

What kind of retirement will this person have ? Not very good . In fact , they will probably have to rely on government subsidies . They will also have to negotiate their debts to the credit card companies to pay them off .

These last few paragraphs sound like the *Paycheck to Paycheck* issues in chapter one , but what I'm getting at is everyone has different assets of value . The very good and not so good .

Now that you know what your total asset is worth , help your spouse or loved one , under the same roof , figure up their total assets . If both of your names are on the mortgage or other deeds, titles or certificates , then this is a shared asset and this will be discussed later in the book . Again , two big assets are obviously better than one in a household . Your going to use your asset reports later on when we lay out your final plans .

With your assets listed before you , please consider the principles listed in chapter one . A 6% investment should have already been started for your retirement , if not , make it a top priority now .

Keep in mind that this is not only for you , but for your spouse and your family . You see... if you have a nice program set up for yourself , your family wont have to worry about you in your retirement years . Mostly , YOU wont have to worry about a retirement income , because if you have been proactive in investing and you have allowed time and money to work for you , the money will be there for you when you need it .

The next step is to protect your families assets ! Do you have an *Advance Directives* form filled out ? A *Living Will* ? An assigned *Power of Attorney* ? A *Last Will and Testament* ? You will need to seriously think about these documents, as these are for your well being and a big relief for your family . You can find these forms in the back of the book for your convenience . Make copies of these forms and assist other family members with their needs.

Your personal documentation , dated , signed and witnessed by non family members or non beneficial persons are important documents in the court of law . One could even video tape themselves on their specific needs or gifts in a will or final wishes .

What would happen if you didn't have these forms filled out ?   Tragedy !

It would be a tragedy if a serious accident or major illness occurred . Maybe your intentions or wishes was other than what you received medically. Or maybe specific gifts was not given to a certain person as you wanted . Or your final resting place was not where you wanted to be .

The possible tragedies could be endless ! Adults can decide for themselves whether they want medical treatment . This right to decide by saying yes or no to proposed treatment , applies to treatments that could extend life , like a breathing machine or a feeding tube . Tragically , an accident or illness can take away a person's ability to make heath care decisions . A decision still has to be made , even if you can not do so , someone else will for you . These decisions should reflect your own values and priorities , your wishes .

Let's discuss each form and see how important it is and how it will protect you and your family .

Advance Directives :   Can be used to name a health care agent . This is someone whom you trust to make health care decisions for you . An advance directive can be used to say what your treatment preferences are , especially about treatments that might be used to sustain your life . The advance directives has two parts , Part A and Part B . You can complete all of the form , or only the parts you want to use . You are not required by law to use these forms . Different forms , written the way you want, may also be used .

These optional forms can be filled out without going to a lawyer . But if there is anything you don't understand or want to add specific details , you may want to talk with a lawyer . You can also ask your doctor to explain the medical issues . You should give a copy of your advance directive to your doctor .

You will need two witnesses to witness your signature on these forms . Nearly any adult can be a witness . If you name a health care , that person may not be a witness . Also , one of the witnesses must be a person who would not financially benefit by your death or handle your estate . You do not need to have the forms notarized .

Advance Directives :   Once you make an advance directive , it remains in effect unless you revoke it. It does not expire . You should review it once in a while , as things may change in your life or your attitudes might change . Be sure to inform your doctor and or anyone else who has a copy of your advance directives if you amend it or revoke it .

You can name anyone you want (except , someone who works for a health care facility where you are receiving care) to be your health care agent . **To name a health care agent , use Part A of the advance directive form .** You can pick a family member as a health care agent , but you don't have to . Remember , your agent will have the power to make important treatment decisions . Choose the person best qualified to be your health care agent . Also consider a back up agent , in case your first choice isn't available . Make sure the person you pick understands what's important to you and when the time comes , do what you would want .

Living Will :   If you want, you can make a limited kind of advance directive called a living will .
A living will lets you decide about life-sustaining procedures in two situations : death from a terminal condition is imminent despite the application of life-sustaining procedures, and a condition of permanent unconsciousness called a persistent vegetative state.

You also have the right to give broader health care instructions by using Part B of the longer form. Part B of the advance directive lets you decide about life-sustaining procedures in three situations : terminal condition, persistent vegetative state, and end-stage condition. An end-stage condition is an advanced, progressive, and incurable condition resulting in complete physical dependency. One example is advanced Alzheimer's disease. You can also use Part B of the advance directive to make health care decisions in addition to those dealing with life-sustaining procedures. If you fill out Part B, you should not fill out the living will form too.

Both the living will form and Part B let you decide separately, if you want, about artificially supplied nutrition and hydration, often called "tube feeding." Also, women who fill out either form can say whether pregnancy is to have any effect on their treatment decisions.

* Fill out, sign, and have witnessed Part A of the advance directive if you want to name a health care agent ?
* Name a back-up agent in case your first choice as health care agent is not available when needed.
* Talk to your agent and back-up agent about your values and priorities, and decide whether that's enough guidance or whether you also want to make specific health care decisions that your agent must follow ?
* Fill out (choosing carefully among alternatives), sign, and have witnessed either a living will or the broader Part B of the advance directive, but only if you want to make specific decisions ?

-18-

* Make sure your health care agent (if you named one), your family, and
your doctor know about your advance care planning ?
* Give a copy of your advance directive to your health care agent, family members,
doctor, and hospital or nursing home if you are a patient there ?

Important Questions you may ask :

1. **Must I use any particular form ?**
   No. Optional forms are provided, but you may change them or use different forms altogether.
   Of course, no health care provider may deny you care simply because you decided not to
   fill out a form.

2. **Who can be picked as a health care agent ?**
   Anyone who is 18 or older except. In general, an owner, operator, or employee of a health
   care facility where a patient is receiving care.

3. **Who can witness an advance directive ?**
   Two witnesses are needed. Generally, any competent adult can be a witness, including
   your doctor or other health care provider (but be aware that some facilities have a
   a policy against their employees serving as witness). If you name a health care agent,
   that person cannot be a witness for any of your advance directives. Also, one of the two
   witnesses must be someone who (I) will not receive money or property from your estate
   and (ii) who is not the one you have named to handle your estate after your death.

4. **Do the forms have to be notarized ?**
   No, but if you travel frequently to another state, check with a knowledgeable lawyer
   to see if that state requires notarization.

5. **Do any of these documents deal with financial matters ?**
   No. If you want to plan for financial matters, talk with your lawyer.

6. **When using these forms to make a decision, how do I show the choices that I have made ?**
   Write your initials next to the statement that says what you want. Don't use checkmarks
   or X's. Then draw lines all the way through other statements that do not say what you want.
   Please don't make inconsistent choices. For example, if you initial any or all of items 1,2,
   and 3 on Part B of the advance directive, do not initial item 5. Draw lines through it instead.
   Also, be very careful about item 4. Draw lines through it if you want to make sure that you
   get pain relief medication.

7. **Should I fill out both the living will form and the advance directive form ?**
   It depends on what you want to do. If all you want to do is name a health care agent, just
   fill out Part A of the advance directive. If you want to give treatment instructions, fill out
   either the living will form or Part B of the advance directive (not both). The living
   will form lets you decide about life-sustaining procedures in the event of terminal condition
   or persistent vegetative state. Part B lets you decide about life sustaining procedures not only
   in the event of terminal condition or persistent vegetative state but also "end -stage condition."
   Part B also lets you make health care decisions that deal with situations other than life-sustaining
   procedures. Be aware that, if you name a health care agent and give treatment instructions, the
   agent will be bound by your decisions unless you say otherwise.

8. **Are these forms valid in another state ?**
   It depends on the law of the other state. Most states will honor an advance directive made
   somewhere else.

9. **To whom should I give copies of my advance directive ?**
   Give copies to your doctor, your health care agent if you name one, hospital or nursing home if
   you will be staying there, and family members or friends who should know of your wishes.

10. **Does the federal law on medical records privacy (HIPAA) require special language about
    my health care agent ?**
    Under HIPAA, a health care agent is a "personal representative" who can get access to your
    medical records. In Part A of the advance directive, at the beginning of item 2A, you might want
    To write in these words: " As my personal representative.... "

11. **If I have an advance directive, do I also need an Emergency Medical Services Palliative
    Care/ Do Not Resuscitate Order ?**
    Yes. If you don't want ambulance personnel to try to resuscitate you in the event of cardiac or
    Respiratory arrest, you must have an EMS palliative Care/ DNR Order signed by your private
    Physician.

12. **Does the EMS Palliative Care/DNR Order have to be in a particular form ?**
    Yes. Ambulance personnel have very little time to evaluate the situation and act appropriately.
    So, it is not practical to ask them to interpret documents that may vary in form and content.
    Instead, a standardized order form has been developed .

13. **Can I use an advance directive to make an organ donation ?**
    Yes. A special form for that purpose is included.

If you have other questions, they may be addressed later on in the book or you may contact your
doctor or lawyer.

Remember when I spoke of a tragedy at the start of this chapter ? I need to share with you a tragedy that occurred a few years ago. This is a true story that will strike home in your heart !

Judy and Fred's parents was divorced . Their mother lived in the same town as the kids and their father lived out of state. As most families go , accounts, investments and retirements are not discussed . Judy and Fred are adults and have their own families to raise , and everybody worked ! Unfortunately , their mother was diagnosed with cancer and a year later , she passed away. She had no will , no retirement and no accounts to speak of , not even life insurance. This awful scenario was left in the children's hands to deal with. The mother had already set up funeral plans prior to her death without paying a dime. Out of their own pockets and help from family and friends was the funeral and burial expenses paid .

Sadly , several years later , their father passed away from prostate cancer . He had previously stated to his children and family , that he had everything taken care of. Also mentioned , a will was made up , accounts secured and properties and possessions was drawn up to be given to his children. His wish was to be cremated and his wife had the ashes shipped to his children . When inquired about the will , the wife stated that there wasn't one ! The children contacted the state county courthouse where he resided to ask if the will or records was there. They stated there was no will or records that pertains to his beneficiaries being Judy or Fred . They received nothing !! Maybe a vase of ashes . Maybe there was a will and it was intentionally destroyed . His wife's telephone number was soon disconnected mysteriously . Their prior relationship was good, not close but good .

How sad is that ??!!

Hence this book was named " Scavengers among us ".

You see , several issues occurred here . A parent should not stick their children with debts or funeral expenses . The children need to speak up and inquire about final arrangements , including wills, accounts and properties . Even if a parent does say its taken care of , one needs to get a copy of the will and other records of concern . If none exists , then plead your case and get things rolling ! We'll discuss this strategy in a later chapter.

Back to the other important forms - an assigned *Power of Attorney* is a very important form which is needed to protect a loved one. A well-drafted power of attorney can avoid the need for a guardianship in most circumstances and save you legal fees . A regular power of attorney gives specific and limited powers (like access to a bank account or permission to sell stock); this power ends if you become incapacitated . A durable power of attorney, however, contains language which makes remain valid even if you become incapacitated . The time an individual will really need a power of attorney is when he or she becomes incompetent . Every older person should have a durable power of attorney for his or her protection.

Here are a few guidelines :
First , give a durable power of attorney to someone whom you can trust with your life. If your not sure about one, consider assigning two people on the power of attorney if your state permits it (regulations on this vary state to state) , so there is some system of checks and balances . Convey your intentions to the agents you appoint in your power of attorney . Make certain they understand your wishes and objectives in your estate and long term care plans. Finally , keep your power of attorney current and up to date . You may want to rewrite it if the status of the assigned power of attorney person changes or a change in your thoughts or influences in your decisions .

Last Will and Testament :
Everyone knows that a Will is an important document to have set up.... to plan ahead. So why is it that so many people put it off ? Could it be that like planning for funeral and burial arrangements , Wills connate death ? Unfortunately , someday we will all have to face it . Death is not a pleasant subject for most people to contemplate . Think about your family for a few seconds..... If you don't have a Will , it is possible that the state could come in and take your assets . Leaving your family without what you had wished they had when you departed . Another sad example is what had happened to Judy and Fred . The end result is NOT what you had wanted !
Remember a Living Will is completely different from a Will and Last Testament . You have property, possessions and assets that you have intentions to give to a loved one or family members . So you will want to list everything you own and seriously contemplate how you wish to disperse your total assets . You may wish a certain person to receive a certain item or the total value of receivable accounts divided equally among family members. A well thought out Will , will have all of your assets listed .

Be sure to make copies of ALL of your documents and give a copy to your P.O.A. , guardian , children , persons of interest , doctor , lawyer , siblings and other concerning members .
The originals should be secured where the person(s) who will need these documents in case of an emergency , will know where to find them . Also consider making a list of all of your important documents and give a list to your spouse , children and executor. The list will include Will , Living Will , P.O.A. , Medical Directives , Organ Donor , Insurances , certificates, titles , deeds , all accounts and holdings in financial institutions , stocks and bonds , personal valuables .
Prepaid accounts like funeral and burial arrangements also should be included .
Exact information like where the items listed can be located , dated and value amount also listed . Someone you trust needs to have access to your records in case of an emergency .

The forms you will need are in the back of this book . Feel free to make copies for yourself and loved ones

Ok... You have given copies, of your plans and wishes, to the ones who need to know. Everyone involved is well informed of their position in your estate or well being .

With everything fresh on your mind , your ready to go into the next chapter .

Chapter Four   What we must do !

Now that you have your family assets and accounts protected , let's think about our parents . If your parents are still alive and have their own assets, properties and accounts , you will need to take a big step here ! We love our parents and the thought of a tragedy striking them is an awful thought ! To lose what they have worked so hard to get and keep up , savings for retirement , etc. .

But this is difficult ! Most older persons don't like to talk about or reveal their assets, properties, possessions . They may feel like someone is trying to get something of theirs . So you will need to explain your own families situation first . How you have everything listed and protected , the proper documents filled out , just in case something should go wrong. One tragedy that could happen is if you should just be driving over to see your parents and be killed in a car accident. Things in life unfortunately do happen. So be passionate and sincere , but don't be pushy. You may feel resistance and they may feel that this may connate being placed in a nursing home or even death. That's alright, give them the time they need . They may say that they will need to talk to someone else about this or to have time to just think about it.

This reminds me of another true story I must share with you ...

An elderly lady was faced with the reality of being unprotected from not having the proper documents . She was aware of the seriousness of this as she had some close friends face the tragedy themselves. When she was offered the documents to get started herself , she stated that she would get them filled out and signed . But never did... When asked later about the documents , again she said she will get them done . Procrastination is what she did . Her family was not prying or trying to get something , they just wanted to protect her and themselves . She had always mentioned that she did not want to be kept alive by breathing and feeding tubes in case something awful happened..
But she had no Living Will form made out. She had mentioned that she wanted her kids to have certain items in the house . But she had no Will made out . She stated she had a burial plot already picked out. But she had no Funeral or Burial plans made out in her Last Testament . Oh... that's right, she doesn't have a Last Testament either. Hopefully she will get all of the documents filled out and signed before anything happens .

If your parents do obliges to filling out all of the documents , ask them to bring out all of their assets, accounts, titles, documents, certificates, deeds and record books. Explain that everything needs to be considered in their Wills and Testament. Review everything and if something doesn't look or sound right, ask the question. If you feel that something needs rewrote or reviewed by a professional, then ask them if you can seek a professional opinion on this one. Maybe an old Will is vague and generic.

If you don't see something that you know they have , ask to see it or help find it , they may think its not important. Don't try to change a beneficiary for them , but if you wonder why one was named, a kind concerned question as to why one was named could be asked.. Remember... this is their choice.

Other important documents are policies and paid receipts for pricy items. Records of money transactions are important : example like Mother loaned her son $3000 , dated and signed by the son on a promise he would pay the money back . But on this date , never have paid it back. Another example would be if a Daughter borrowed a $12000 diamond necklace and to date has not returned it. Be sure to have accurate records dated, items listed, values, names, signed and even witnessed if possible. Its awful that a parent has to do this , but if not , something could turn sour . If the children involved understands and is sincere about returning the transaction, then there is no hard feelings. This is called protection ! Now a days , you have to protect yourself !

Taking pictures or a video of their possessions and properties is also a wise thing to do. This will show what they own, along with dates and values listed. Also if a parent wants a certain item to go to a child , then write the name of the beneficiary on the photo . This also is wise protection in case of a fire, weather emergency loss or burglary . A video is very good too , in that it shows what is in place in a home that the owners rarely rearrange furniture or possessions . If an item comes up missing, review the video ! Although these pictures and video should be locked up in a bank lock box due to the possible tragedies mentioned. .

Another point of interest is if say your Father remarried and his wife brought into the marriage assets. Accurate records are needed here ! Records of what the asset is, date , value, names related to the asset and information tagged on the asset . List a persons own accounts , like not joint accounts. List joint accounts separately. Record any personal estates, investments and gifts with accurate information. Again , consider and list everything : assets, accounts, monies, retirements, incomes now to date, certificates, policies , stocks, bonds, personal possessions and properties . Beneficiaries will need to be assigned to each asset just mentioned .

This could take hours to cover everything , so you may want to do this over several days . Just be sure to have the Living Will, Will and Last Testament , POA , Medical Directives and Organ donor (If interested) completely filled out , dated and signed. Copies given to respected persons . Originals given to a trusted POA or lawyer .

Chapter Five   Let's have a Heart to Heart talk

A very trusting, but scarey thing to do !! Your POA can be a very trusted child of yours, who has all of their heart into the care of their parent - close to the last five to seven years before the parent will have to go into the nursing home (if that is the choice of care), transfer 75% of the total bank accounts into the POA's name. Yes.. I know .. It does sound crazy and scarey , but there is a simple explanation to this.

Understand the Medicaid law and you will know where I'm coming from.
To be able to get Medicaid financial assistance to pay for the nursing home , a person's accounts will need to be liquidated down to a bare minimum. Sad , but true... if your Father has worked hard all of his life and has in bank accounts, say $300,000 total , the Medicaid program says by law that he must pay for his nursing home expenses or he must spend half of the total value ($150,000) , on his home or properties or vehicles - NOT give it away to is children in gifts or vacations or cash.

Not knowing when one will go into the Nursing home is difficult , but seven years is safe, if he transfers the money into a trust account in his POA's name , then the money is not tied to the Father. All of his accounts at the time of admission into a home will show he has only $75,000 in his name, to which the nursing home will use to pay for the monthly care, down to $1500. Then Medicaid will then step in upon application. He could put 90% into his POA's trust account , leaving the Father $30,000 in his name. This $30,000 sounds better than $75,000 going into a nursing care.

Now let's understand again that this is a trusted POA child of the Father. All of this money is going into a trust account under the name of the POA. If the Father wants money for any reason , alright , as its really his money - NOT the POA's. The POA has no right to the money , as it is in a trust.
Also if there are other siblings or close family members , they can help over see this trust account, knowing that this trust is held in high regards for their Father. The POA can also reassure the Father and other close family members by showing a bank account statement once in awhile to them , that the trust account is actual and growing with interest. Its only fair to do this !

Under sworn secrecy and trust will this work in a close family. Would the Father rather pay the nursing home the $300,000 or let his family be beneficiaries to most of the money ?
Also in this trust is a sworn statement that if the Father should pass away , the POA will equally share the trust account with other siblings or family members, or as stated in a secret trust letter like a Will - as to what the Fathers wishes are to dispersing the trust account funds.

This trust account is a family secret and is NOT to be revealed to anyone !

This is NOT a dishonest transaction ! The parents would have wanted the children to benefit from the monies left after they pass away . This money transaction thought actually came from two different lawyers I personally have pursued for legal work for my own Father.

Here is another side of the coin. If your parent (s) are NOT going to a nursing home and plan to live out their own home with maybe home health care , then consider this again.

Discuss the possibility of where they might be in seven years , if there is a chance that they may have to go to a nursing home in seven years or soon after , then the trust transaction should take place.

I had wished that with my own Father , I had known this information ten years ago . My siblings and I would have secured accurate records , recorded pertinent information, have documents dated and signed, even tried to pursue the trust transaction with the POA. As I had mentioned early in the book, when a mother-in-law and her children played a big part in legal issues on health issues , accurate records on who brought what into the marriage and other important documents are essential legal records. No one knows what may happen ten - twenty years from a very happy, loving relationship. Even a whole happy family relationship including step children and grandchildren can turn sour and ugly in the court of law.

A common mistake is thinking a bank account is secured from scavengers . If large bank accounts was to be placed into a 401K , IRA or a company retirement program , it would be safer than a bank account .

While getting your parents documents all set up , dated and signed - be sure that the Will states that it MAY NOT be contested by anyone. That this a true and accurate testament dated and sign by _____ . Witnessed by _____ and _____ .

Having a Notary Public witness, date, signed and stamped is also recommended.

Be patient and work with them on this lengthily family documentation process.

Reassure them that this is what you and your family went through , and legal resources do stress that all families need to be protected with proper documentation .

A few final thoughts : If your parents must leave the home for Assisted Living or Nursing Home Care , the POA should change the locks on the home , in case other people may have a key to get into the home. This is to keep honest people honest ! Valuable papers like mortgage , CD's, deed , account books , Wills, policies, titles , etc. should be secured in a bank lock box.

Valuable possessions like guns, jewelry, coins, heirlooms , etc. should be secured in another safe place when no one is living there in the home. If the possessions are in a persons safe place , there should be a list of the transaction , dated and signed - so the family that has interest knows where and what is being secured for safe keeping. Then if later on, another disbursement will be taking place like in a Will , then all on the secured list will be brought out legally.

No one knows how a person will be drawing up their Will , but hopefully it will be fair to their children. But its been known that one will receive a large gift and another nothing , sad but true. Relationships , good or not so good can end up different results .

Here is a final true story :

A country lady I knew , lived close to her Mother and Father . Her brother lived several miles away. Suddenly the Mother passed away unexpectedly . A few months later the Father passed away also. Totally shocked to the parents passing as the family was very close . The daughter and her brother had another brother who had passed away years prior to this. The deceased brothers children contested the Will of their Grand parents . Stating that they should be entitled to their fathers part. Although there was NO WILL , they secured an attorney to contest and won their part. They received a lake front cottage and furnishings valued at $120,000 . The whole total assets was appraised and each child received a third of the total. The lake cottage was enjoyed by the whole family , but because the home this Lady lived in was a part of the estate , she was afraid she could lose her home.

The Brother received the home the parents lived in , which in turn he gave to his son and his family, as he already had a nicer home he presently lived in . The acreage was divided equally between the sister and brother , making their share more valuable. The out come was unpleasant to the sister and brother , as the deceased brothers children didn't really have a close relationship with their grand parents .

If the Mother and Father had a Will and kept it up to date , maybe the out come would have been more favorable for the sister and brother , who was very close to their parents . They visited and cared for them everyday ! The grand children rarely visited . Another sad story !

Even other family members , grand children or step children may intervene and contest a Will . A person or persons can take advantage of a situation to gang financial
satisfaction .

So one should state in their Will that it will NOT be contested by anyone. Signed , dated and witnessed by two non-interested persons. Non-interested means that they have no part or interest in the estate of the Will .

May the information I have given you be of high value to you and your family . I wish that everyone can understand the legal reasoning behind the documents and the trust account in the name of the POA.

Yes... that is a big transaction for anyone to take. If one would seriously think about it, more than likely the children will benefit the money anyway , after the parent passes away. Although there are rare stories where the children receive only a few possessions and someone else or an organization receives a large sum of money .

My personal thought is if I get to an age where I am not able to go on vacations anymore , don't care to go anywhere but my home , have everything I need , don't feel as well as I use to , I live off of my social security and retirement , everything is paid off and I really don't need $ 300,000 growing in a bank..... I can give my child , my POA , a trust account in his name only. She/he will agree and sign a trust document stating that this trust account is my money and it is being held in trust in the name of my child . If I need any of the money I can get it at any time from my POA. I will look at this seven years before I feel I will have to go into a nursing home and while I still have my mental capacity to legally sign a document .

I would be happy to keep 10% of the total , which is $30,000 . Then I can pay the nursing home each month from this $30,000 account (that's all the money I own) until it gets down to $1500 , then Medicaid will need to be applied for to pay for the Nursing Care .

Sounds good to me !   Think about it !

Tim Wentz

Advance Directive

Part A
Appointment of Health - care Agent
(*Optional Form*)

(Cross through this whole part of the form if you do not want to appoint a health care agent to make health care decisions for you. If you do want to appoint an agent, cross through any items in the form that you do not want to apply.)

1. I _____ , residing at

   _____

   _____

   Appoint the following individual as my agent to make health care decisions for me :

   _____

   _____

   (Full Name, Address, and Telephone Number of Agent)

   Optional : If this agent is unavailable or is unable or unwilling to act as my agent , then I
   Appoint the following person to act I this capacity :

   _____

   _____

   (Full Name, Address, and Telephone Number of Back - up Agent)

2. My Agent has full power and authority to make health care decisions for me, including the Power to :
   A. Request , receive , and review any information, oral or written, regarding my physical or Mental health, including, but not limited to, medical and hospital records, and consent to Disclosure of this information.

   B. Employ and Discharge my health care providers.

   C. Authorize my admission to or discharge from (including transfer to another facility) any hospital , hospice, nursing home, adult home, or other medical facility; and

   D. Consent to the provision, withholding, or withdrawal of health care, including, in Appropriate circumstances, life sustaining procedures.

3. The authority of my agent is subject to the following provisions and limitations :

    _____

    _____

4. If I am pregnant , my agent shall follow these specific instructions :

    _____

    _____

5. My agent's authority becomes operative (initial only the one option that applies):

    _____   When my attending physician and a second physician determine that I am incapable
                  of making an informed decision regarding my health care : or

    _____   When this document is signed .

6. My agent is to make health care decisions for me based on the health care instructions I give in
    this document and on my wishes as otherwise known to my agent. If my wishes are unknown
    or unclear , my agent is to make health care decisions for me in accordance with my best
    interest , to be determined by my agent after considering the benefits, burdens, and risks that
    might result from a given treatment of course of treatment, or from the withholding or
    withdrawal of a treatment or course of treatment.

7. My agent shall not be liable for the costs of care based solely on this authorization.

By signing below, I indicate that I am emotionally and mentally competent to make this appointment
of a health care agent and that I understand its purpose and effect.

_____   _____
     (Date)   (signature of Declaring person)

The Declaring person signed or acknowledged signing this appointment of a health care agent in my
presence and based upon my personal observation, appears to be a competent individual.

_____   _____
     (Witness)   (Witness)

_____   _____

_____   _____

                    (Signatures and Addresses of Two Witnesses)

Advance Directive

Part B
Health Care Instructions
(Optional Form)

(Cross through this whole part of the form if you do not want to give health care instructions .
If you do want to complete this portion of the form, initial those statements you want to be included
in the document and cross through those statements that do not apply.)

If I am incapable of making an informed decision regarding my health care, I direct my health care
providers to follow my instructions as set forth below. (initial all those that apply)

1. If my death from a terminal condition is imminent and even if life-sustaining procedures are
    used there is no reasonable expectations of my recovery :

    _____ I direct that my life not be extended by life-sustaining procedures, including
    the administration of nutrition and hydration artificially .

    _____ I direct that my life not be extended by life-sustaining procedures, except
    that if I am unable to take food by mouth, I wish to receive nutrition and
    hydration artificially.

2. If I am in a persistent vegetative state, that is, if I am not conscious and am not aware of my
    environment nor able to interact with others, and there is no reasonable expectation of my
    recovery :

    _____ I direct that my life not be extended by life-sustaining procedures, including
    the administration of nutrition and hydration artificially.

    _____ I direct that my life not be extended by life-sustaining procedures, except
    that if I am unable to take food by mouth, I wish to receive nutrition and
    hydration artificially.

3. If I have an end-stage condition, that is, a condition caused by injury, disease , or illness, as a
    result of which I have suffered severe and permanent deterioration indicated by incompetency
    and complete physical dependency and for which, to a reasonable degree of medical certainty,
    treatment of the irreversible condition would be medically ineffective :

    _____ I direct that my life not be extended by life-sustaining procedures,
    including the administration of nutrition and hydration artificially.

    _____ I direct that my life not to be extended by life-sustaining procedures,
    except that I am unable to take food and water by mouth, I wish to
    receive nutrition and hydration artificially.

4. _____ I direct that, no matter what my condition, medication to relieve pain and suffering not be given to me if the medication would shorten my remaining life.

5. _____ I direct that, no matter what my condition, I be given all available medical treatment in accordance with accepted health care standards.

6. If I am pregnant, my decision concerning life-sustaining procedures shall be modified as follows:

_____

_____

7. I direct (in the following space, indicating any other instructions regarding receipt or nonreceipt of any health care) :

_____

_____

_____

By signing below, I indicate that I am emotionally and mentally competent to make this Advance Directive and that I understand the purpose and effect of this document.

_____   _____
(Date)   (Signature of Declaring person)

The Declarant signed or acknowledged signing these health care instructions in my presence and based upon my personal observation, appears to be a competent individual.

_____   _____
(Witness)   (Witness)

_____   _____

_____   _____

_____   _____

(Signatures and Addresses of two Witnesses)

Durable power of Attorney

ATTORNEY IN FACT

I , _____ hereby create a durable power of Attorney, "Power" and appoint the following person(s) as my Attorney In Fact, in the order in which their names appear, with power to act for me according to state code 30-5-5, as it now exists or as it may be amended in the future, excluding state code 30-5-5-16 and 30-5-5-17.

_____

_____

A successor Attorney In Fact shall be replaced as provided in section 4 and the next successor Attorney In Fact, in the order named above, shall replace and succeed the applicable to my Attorney In Fact.

A. Powers

I give Attorney In Fact , including any successor Attorney In Fact, the powers contained in this power. These powers are granted upon the condition they will be used for my benefit and on my behalf and will be exercised only in a fiduciary capacity.

(1) TRUST AGREEMENT. Authority with respect to delivering and conveying my assets to the then Trustee of any Trust executed by me, as the same may be amended from time to time before my death ;
(2) REAL PROPERTY . Authority with respect to real property Transactions;
(3) TANGIBLE PERSONAL PROPERTY . Authority with respect to tangible personal property transactions;
(4) BOND, SHARE, AND COMMODITY . Authority with respect to bond, share and commodity transactions. This authority includes the power to purchase United States Government obligations which are redeemable at par in payment of estate taxes imposed by the United States Government;
(5) BANKING . Authority with respect to banking transactions, including but not limited to, the authority to have access to any and all safety deposit boxes in my name, and to open, inspect, inventory, place items in or remove items from and close safety deposit boxes ;
(6) BUSINESS . Authority with respect to business operating transactions;
(7) INSURANCE . Authority with respect to insurance transactions, including full power to apply for and otherwise deal with medicare and medicaid benefits;
(8) BENEFICIARY . Authority with respect to beneficiary transactions.
(9) GIFTS . Authority with respect to gift transactions, without regard to any limits on dollar amounts and without any prohibition against self-dealing except as provided below ;
(10) FIDUCIARY . Authority with respect to fiduciary transactions;
(11) CLAIMS AND LITIGATION . Authority with respect to claims and litigation ;
(12) ESTATE TRANSACTIONS . Authority with respect to estate transactions;
(13) ALL OTHER MATTERS . Authority with respect to all other possible matters and affairs affecting property owned by me. Notwithstanding the foregoing, in no event shall my Attorney In Fact have any of the following power :
    (a) To benefit himself, herself, or any other person in any way that could result in any part

of my property being included in my Attorney In Fact's gross estate for federal estate tax purposes, or cause any part of my property to be deemed to be the subject of a taxable gift made personally by Attorney In Fact :

(b) To make any payment, or application which discharged any legal obligation of mu Attorney In Fact :

(c) To possess the power to exercise any incident of ownership with respect to any policy I own insuring the life of my Attorney In Fact :

(d) To have any power which causes the hold of power to be treated as the owner of any interest in my property and which causes that property to be taxed as owned by the Attorney In Fact :

I ratify and confirm all that my Attorney In Fact does, or causes to be done, under the authority granted in this Power. All documents signed, endorsed, drawn, accepted, made, executed, or delivered by my Attorney In Fact shall bind me, my heirs, successors and assigns.

IN WITNESS WHEREOF , I have hereunto set my hand and seal on this _____ day of
_____ month, _____ year.

_____
(signature of claimant / owner)

STATE OF _____
COUNTY OF _____

On this _____ day of _____ month , _____ year,

before me, a Notary Public in and for this County, personally appeared _____
to me known to be the person described in and who executed the within instrument and who acknowledged the same to be his free act and deed. Hereby witnessed and notarized.

_____
Printed :
Notary Public, _____ County,

State of _____ .

My Commission expires _____

Power of Attorney

Taxpayer(s) name, relationship to decedent, and address including ZIP code (Please type or print)

_____

_____

Hereby appoints (name(s), address(es), including ZIP code(s), and telephone number(s) of Individual(s)

_____

_____

_____

As attorney(s)-in-fact to represent the taxpayer(s) before the Inheritance Tax Division of the State Department of Revenue in all tax matters concerning the estate of

_____ who died a resident of

_____ county in the state of _____ .

The estate was opened in the _____ court under

Cause Number _____ . The decedent's date of death is

_____ .

The attorney(s)-in-fact (or either of them) are authorized, subject to revocation, to receive confidential information and to perform any and all acts that the principal(s) can perform with respect to the above specified tax matters (excluding the power to receive refund checks, and the power to sign the return, unless specifically granted below).

Send copies of notices and other written communications addressed to the taxpayer(s) in proceeding involving the above tax matters to :
1. The appointee first named above, or
2. (Names of not more than two of the above named appointees) _____

initial here _____ if you are granting the power to receive, but not to endorse or cash, refund checks for the above tax matters to :
3. The appointee first named above, or
4. (Names of one of the above designated appointees) _____

This power of attorney revokes all earlier powers of attorney and tax information authorizations on file with the Inheritance Tax Division of the State Department of Revenue for the same tax maters covered by this power of attorney, except the following :

_____

_____

(Specify to whom granted, date and address of earlier powers and authorizations.)

Signatures of or for taxpayer(s)
(If signed by a fiduciary on behalf of the taxpayer, I certify that I have the authority to execute this
    Power of attorney on behalf of the taxpayer.)

_____   _____   _____
      (Signature)   (Title)   (Date)

(Also pe or print your name below if signing for a taxpayer who is not an individual.)

_____   _____   _____
      (Signature)   (Title)   (Date)

My Personal - Will and Last Testament

I drew up my own Will and Last Testament because I felt the example shown in the previous form was too vague. It would be fine for a person who has very little to leave to a family member or two and who doesn't have a complicated relationship where he/she has personal assets , joint assets and step children or involved family members.

I have found personally that one needs to record every asset and keep accurate records and receipts, so that if a sad scenario does occur in our later years, it is properly recorded with proof of receipt and then the attorneys wont have to dispute over logistics.

So record first what you have brought into a marriage and record what she brought in and then what you jointly have together. Record your incomes and then hers and then jointly what is accountable and disbursed , like annual incomes and who pays for what or amount paid into a joint account and what is paid out of that account for what purpose. Properties and personal possessions will need to be recorded also the same way - who owns what, value, dates, receipts and if jointly owned- listed as such.

Be sure to list ALL assets like Insurances, stocks, bonds, other accounts, deeds, titles and certificates. If a lawyer would have to read your Will and Last Testament , there would not be anything of value left out to disbursed . Also beneficiaries wont have to dispute anything if it is drawn up correctly and all spelled out.

Beneficiaries assigned to certain accounts , properties and personal possessions should have been thought out throughly on the assignments. Example would be like your husband will receive 80% of an account and then each child of two will receive 10% each.

Outstanding debts should also be listed , as of a date and balance of the account(s) .

I feel it also should be recorded , that your Will and Last Testament is a true , accurate wish of yours and that it is NOT to be disputed - signed and dated with two witnesses not related to you and not having an interest in your estate.

Your final arrangement plans and resting place needs to be listed exactly as you wish. All debts and accounts to these plans should be prepaid by you or out of an account set up for your final plans. Example could be your wish to be cremated , no public services held, family and friends will come together for a party to celebrate your life , with aunt Betty Johnson singing hymns and brother Joe Smith reading a personal message from you.

Copies of your Will and Last Testament given to Beneficiaries . The original is secured by your lawyer or POA who is trusted person in your best interest. A video of you stating exactly what you wish in your Will and Last Testament would be a strong legal tool, this also will need to be secured for the final reading.

Don't leave anything of value out of your Will and Last Testament. If assets change or people of interest change , update your final wishes . Be sure to make changes while you are still legally competent to do so. If you are in your senior years, you may need to have a physician to evaluate and sign off that you are competent to record and sign documents.

Sincerely , Tim Wentz   June 17th, 2008

Last Will and Testament
Of

_____

I, _____ , of _____ county ,

_____ state , being of sound and disposing mind and memory, do make, publish and declare this to be my Last Will and Testament, and revoke all other wills and codicils that I may have made.

ITEM I . I direct that all my just debts, including the expenses of mt last illness and funeral, all inheritance, estate and succession taxes payable by reason of my death shall be paid out of my estate by my Execut(or/rix) or as soon as practicable after the time of decease .

ITEM II. All the rest, residue and remainder of my estate, real and personal, of which I may die seized or possessed, or to which I may be entitled, I devise and bequeath unto my _____ , _____ , to be(hers, his, theirs) absolutely.

ITEM III. In the event that my _____ , _____ , shall have predeceased me or died simultaneously or in a common disaster with me, then I devise and bequeath my entire estate, real, personal and mixed of which I may die seized or possessed or to which I may be entitled, unto my _____ , _____ , to be (hers, his, absolutely or divided equally) .

ITEM IV . I hereby make, nominate and appoint my _____ , _____ , to be the Execut(or/rix). Of this my Last Will and Testament, hereby authorizing and empowering my said Execut(or/rix) to compound, compromise, settle and adjust all claims and demands in favor of or against my estate; and to sell, at private or public sale, at such prices, and upon such terms of credit or otherwise, as (he/she/ they) may deem best, the whole or any part of my real or personal property, and to execute, acknowledge and deliver deeds and other proper instruments of conveyance thereof to the purchaser or purchasers. I request that no bond be required of my said Execut(r/rix). In the event that my _____ , _____ , shall have predeceased me or (is/are) unable to serve as Execut(or/rix) for any reason, then in such event, I make, nominate and appoint my _____ , _____ , to be the second Execut(or/rix) of this my Last Will and Testament, conferring upon _____ the same authority and powers as expressed here in above .

IN WITNESS WHEREOF , I have hereunto set my hand this _____ day of

_____ month , _____ year .

_____
(signature of creator   )

Health care Representative Appointment

1. I , _____ of
    (Name of principal)

    _____
    (address)

    Hereby appoint _____
    (Name of health care representative)

    of _____
    (address and telephone number)

    as my health care representative .

2. In the event the person I appoint above is unable, unwilling or unavailable to act as my

    health care representative , I hereby appoint _____
    (Name of successor health care representative)

    of _____
    (address and telephone number)

3. I authorize my health care representative and my successor health care representative to
    make decisions in my best interest concerning my health care, including consent to health
    care as well as withdrawal or withholding of health care. Pursuant to the Health Care
    Consent Act, I authorize my health care representative and my successor health care
    representative to make decisions to withhold or withdraw artificial nutrition and hydration
    to the extent it is in my best interest to do so. If at any time , based on my previously
    expressed preferences and the diagnosis and prognosis, my health care representative or
    successor health care representative is satisfied that certain health care is not or would not
    be beneficial, or that such health care is or would be excessively burdensome, then my
    health care representative or successor health care representative may express my will that
    such health care be withheld or withdrawn and may consent on my behalf that any or all
    health care be discontinued or not instituted, even if death may result.

    My health care representative or successor health care representative must try to discuss
    this decision with me. However, if I am unable to communicate, my health care
    representative or successor health care representative may make such a decision for me,
    after consultation with my physician or physicians and other relevant health care givers.
    To the extent appropriate, my health care representative may also discuss this decision
    with my family and others, to the extent they are available .

_____   _____
(Date)   (Name of Principal)

Organ donation addendum

Note : If you want to be an organ donor , you can attach this page to your living will or advance
directive . Sign it and have it witnessed .

Upon my death, I wish to donate :

_____   Any needed organs, tissues or eyes.

_____   Only the following organs, tissues, or eyes :

_____

_____

I authorize the use of y organs, tissues, or eyes :

_____   For transplantation :
_____   For therapy :
_____   For research :
_____   For medical education :
_____   For any purpose authorized by law .

I understand that before any vital organ, tissue or eye may be removed for transplantation,
I must be pronounced dead. After death, I direct that all support measures be continued to
maintain the viability for transplantation of my organs, tissues, and eyes until organ, tissue and
eye recovery has been completed .

I understand that my estate will not be charged for any costs associated with my decision to
donate my organs , tissues , and eyes or the actual disposition of my organs, tissues, and eyes.

By signing below , I indicate that I am emotionally and mentally competent to make this
organ donation addendum and that I understand the purpose and effect of this document.

_____   _____
      (Date)   (Signature of Declarant)

The Declarant signed or acknowledged signing this organ donation addendum in my
presence and based upon my personal observation appears to be a competent individual.

_____   _____
      (Witness)   (Witness)

_____   _____

(Signature of Two Witnesses)

www.ingramcontent.com/pod-product-compliance
Lightning Source LLC
Chambersburg PA
CBHW081232020426
42331CB00012B/3138